IT'S ALL ABOUT WATER

PAGE PUBLISHING
Conneaut Lake, PA

First originally published by Page Publishing 2023

ISBN 979-8-88654-484-8 (pbk)
ISBN 979-8-88654-487-9 (digital)

Printed in the United States of America

IT'S ALL ABOUT WATER

Celeste Adams Wells Alexander, Ed.S

I drink water.

The formula for water is H2O:

(2) two hydrogens and (1) one oxygen.

Water is made up of (2) two elements: hydrogen and oxygen, which can be found on the Periodic Table.

Hydrogen has an atomic number of (1) one, and its symbol is H.

Oxygen has an atomic number of 8 (eight), and its symbol is O.

Water is a compound because it consists of (2) two or more elements.

Element Key

1
H
HYDROGEN
1.008
ATOMIC NUMBER
- Number of electrons
- Number of protons
SYMBOL
NAME
ATOMIC MASS
-In AMU
(Atomic Mass Units)

Element Key

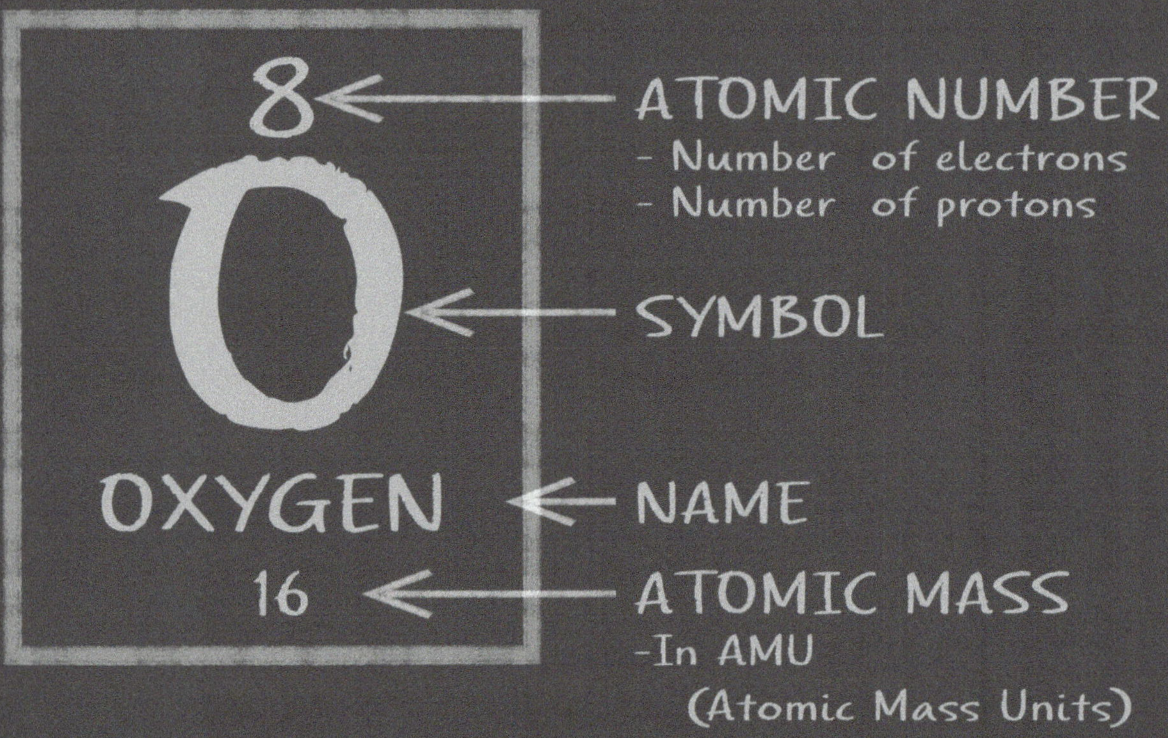

8 ← ATOMIC NUMBER
- Number of electrons
- Number of protons

O ← SYMBOL

OXYGEN ← NAME

16 ← ATOMIC MASS
-In AMU
(Atomic Mass Units)

Periodic Table of the Elements

Group headings (top): 1 IA 1A; 2 IIA 2A; 3 IIIB 3B; 4 IVB 4B; 5 VB 5B; 6 VIB 6B; 7 VIIB 7B; 8, 9, 10 VIII; 11 IB 1B; 12 IIB 2B; 13 IIIA 3A; 14 IVA 4A; 15 VA 5A; 16 VIA 6A; 17 VIIA 7A; 18 VIIIA 8A.

Key box:
- Atomic Number (top left), Boiling Point (top right)
- Symbol
- Name
- Atomic Mass

Notes:
- Normal boiling points are in °C
- SP = Triple Point
- Pressure is listed if not 1 atm.
- Allotrope is listed if more than one allotrope.

Z	Boiling Point	Symbol	Name	Atomic Mass
1	-252.762	H	Hydrogen	1.008
2	-268.93	He	Helium	4.003
3	1342	Li	Lithium	6.941
4	2471	Be	Beryllium	9.012
5	4000	B	Boron	10.811
6	graphite 38.25 SP	C	Carbon	12.011
7	-195.798	N	Nitrogen	14.007
8	-182.953	O	Oxygen	18.999
9	-188.12	F	Flourine	18.998
10	-246.053	Ne	Neon	20.180
11	882.940	Na	Sodium	22.990
12	1090	Mg	Magnesium	24.305
13	2519	Al	Aluminum	26.982
14	3625	Si	Silicon	28.086
15	-0000	P	Phosphorus	30.974
16	444.61	S	Sulfur	32.066
17	-101.5	Cl	Chlorine	35.453
18	-185.847	Ar	Argon	35.948
19	759	K	Potassium	39.098
20	1484	Ca	Calcium	40.078
21	2836	Sc	Scandium	44.956
22	3287	Ti	Titanium	47.88
23	3407	V	Vanadium	50.942
24	2671	Cr	Chromium	51.996
25	2061	Mn	Manganese	54.938
26	2861	Fe	Iron	55.933
27	2927	Co	Cobalt	59.933
28	2913	Ni	Nickel	59.693
29	2562	Cu	Copper	63.546
30	907	Zn	Zinc	65.39
31	2204	Ga	Gallium	39.732
32	2833	Ge	Germanium	72.61
33	616 SP	As	Arsenic	74.922
34	685	Se	Selenium	78.972
35	-0000	Br	Bromine	79.904
36	-0000	Kr	Krypton	84.80
37	688	Rb	Rubidium	84.468
38	1382	Sr	Strontium	87.62
39	3345	Y	Yttrium	88.906
40	4409	Zr	Zirconium	91.224
41	4744	Nb	Niobium	92.906
42	4639	Mo	Molybdenum	95.95
43	4265	Tc	Technetium	98.907
44	4150	Ru	Ruthenium	101.07
45	3695	Rh	Rhodium	102.906
46	2963	Pd	Palladium	106.42
47	2162	Ag	Silver	1007.868
48	767	Cd	Cadmium	112.411
49	2072	In	Indium	114.818
50	2602	Sn	Tin	118.71
51	1587	Sb	Antimony	121.760
52	988	Te	Tellurium	127.6
53	-0000	I	Iodine	126.904
54	-0000	Xe	Xenon	131.29
55	671	Cs	Cesium	132.905
56	1897	Ba	Barium	137.327
57-71				
72	4603	Hf	Hafnium	178.49
73	5458	Ta	Tantalum	180.948
74	5555	W	Tungsten	183.85
75	5596	Re	SAMPLE	182
76	5012	Os	Osmium	190.23
77	4428	Ir	Iridium	192.22
78	3825	Pt	Platinum	195.08
79	2856	Au	Gold	196.967
80	356.62	Hg	Mercury	200.59
81	1473	Tl	Thallium	204.383
82	1749	Pb	Lead	207.2
83	1564	Bi	Bismuth	208.980
84	962	Po	Polonium	[208.982]
85	-0000	At	Astatine	209.987
86	-61.7	Rn	Radon	222.018
87	677	Fr	Francium	223.020
88	1737	Ra	Radium	226.025
89-103				
104	unknown	Rf	Rutherfordium	[261]
105	unknown	Db	Dubnium	[262]
106	unknown	Sg	Seaborgium	[266]
107	unknown	Bh	Bohrium	[264]
108	unknown	Hs	Hassium	[269]
109	unknown	Mt	Meitnerium	[268]
110	unknown	Ds	Darmstadtium	[269]
111	unknown	Rg	Roentgenium	[272]
112	unknown	Cn	Copernicium	[277]
113	unknown	Uut	Ununtrium	unknown
114	unknown	Fl	Flerovium	[289]
115	unknown	Uup	Ununpentium	unknown
116	unknown	O	SAMPLE	182
117	unknown	Uus	Ununseptium	unknown
118	unknown	Uuo	Ununoctium	unknown

Lanthanide Series

Z	Boiling Point	Symbol	Name	Atomic Mass
57	3464	La	Lanthanum	138.906
58	3443	Ce	Cerium	140.115
59	3520	Pr	Praseodymium	140.908
60	3074	Nd	Neodymium	144.24
61	3000	Pm	Promethium	144.913
62	1794	Sm	Samarium	150.36
63	1529	Eu	Europium	151.966
64	3273	Gd	Gadolinium	157.25
65	3230	Tb	Terbium	158.925
66	2567	Dy	Dysprosium	162.50
67	2700	Ho	Holmium	164.930
68	2868	Er	Erbium	164.930
69	1950	Tm	Thulium	168.934
70	1196	Yb	Ytterbium	173.04
71	3402	Lu	Lutetium	174.967

Actinide Series

Z	Boiling Point	Symbol	Name	Atomic Mass
89	3198	Ac	Actinium	227.028
90	-0000	Th	Thorium	232.038
91	4027	Pa	Protactinium	231.036
92	4131	U	Uranium	238.029
93	4174	Np	Neptunium	237.048
94	3228	Pu	Plutonium	244.064
95	2011	Am	Americium	243.061
96	3100	Cm	Curium	247.070
97	2627	Bk	Berkelium	247.070
98	unknown	Cf	Californium	251.080
99	unknown	Es	Einsteinium	[254]
100	unknown	Fm	Fermium	257.095
101	unknown	Md	Mendelevium	258.1
102	unknown	No	Nobelium	259.101
103	unknown	Lr	Lawrencium	[262]

Legend: Alkali Metal · Alkaline Earth · Transition Metal · Basic Metal · Semimetal · Nonmetal · Halogen · Noble Gas · Lanthanide · Actinide

The water we drink is fresh water. It comes from lakes, rivers, streams, groundwater, etc. It has less than 1% salt (NaCl), which is a compound. Can you name the elements in salt?

Water is recycled and has been around along time.
It probably rolled down a dinosaur's back.

Water goes from the atmosphere to the earth and back again. This is called the water cycle.

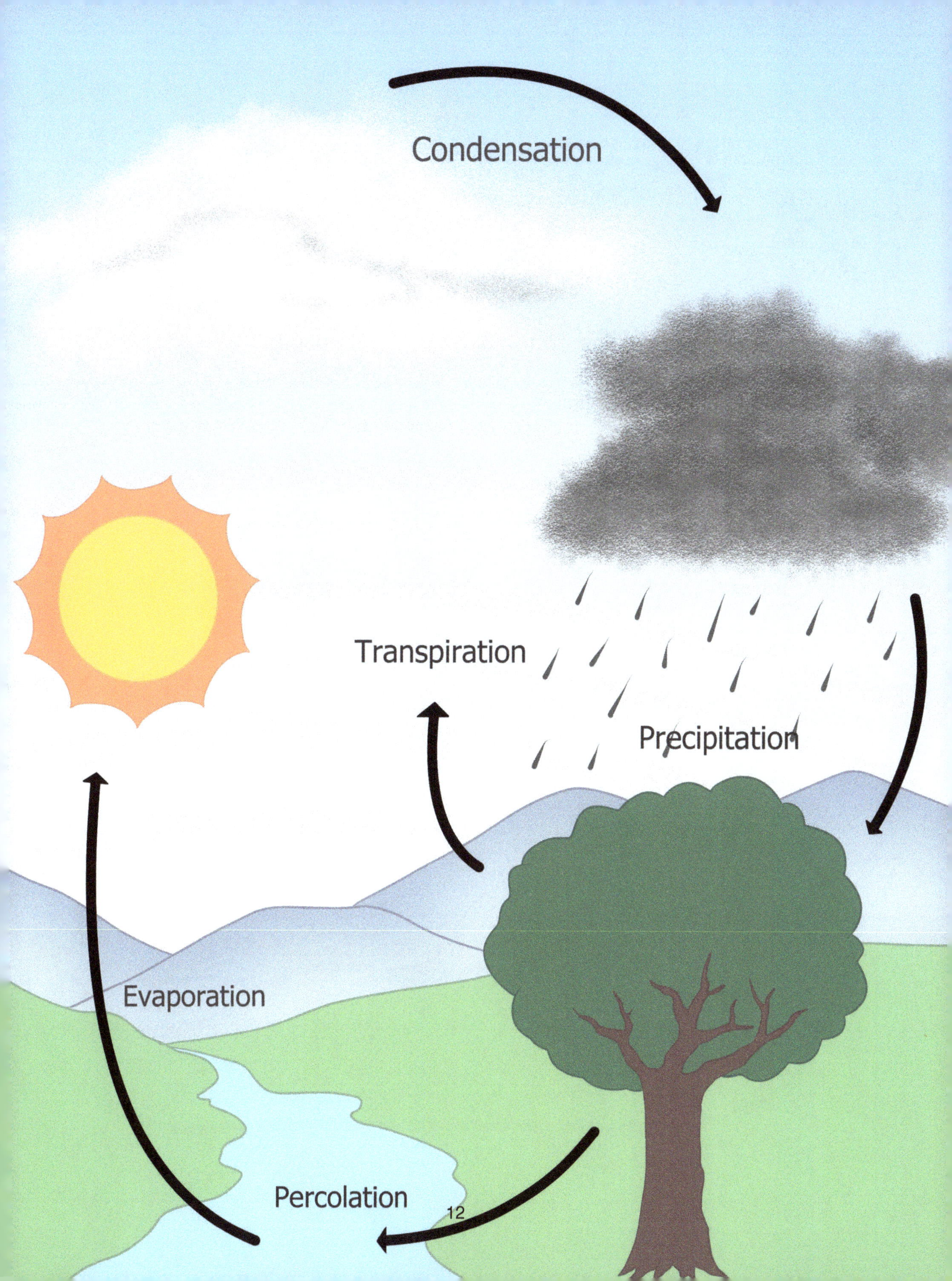

Condensation
Transpiration
Precipitation
Evaporation
Percolation
12

Water has three phases, which
are solid, liquid, and gas.

Solid: ice

Liquid: water

Gas: steam

Water is essential to life here on earth. Imagine how earth would look without water. Plants and animals need water to live. It's all about water. What did you learn today about water?

So drink up. It's only water.

Questions

Water is a/an
- a. compound
- b. element
- c. symbol

Hydrogen is a/an
- a. compound
- b. element
- c. symbol

Oxygen is a/an
- a. compound
- b. element
- c. symbol

What is the water cycle?

Can you name the phase of water when it is solid?

About the Author

Celeste Ann Adams Wells Alexander is the daughter of the late Rev. C. O. Adams Sr. and Mrs. Gladys Myrick Adams. Celeste Alexander's siblings include Carolyn Adams, Rev. C. Otis Adams Jr., and the late Clover Adams. She was married to the late Rev. Charles E. Wells Jr. She is currently married to the Rev. Keith Alexander Sr.

Celeste is a retired science teacher with thirty years of teaching experience in public schools and juvenile detention. She has a bachelor of science degree, a master of science degree, and an education specialist degree. The colleges and universities attended are Morris Brown College, Georgia State University, Troy State University, and Capella University.

Mrs. Alexander was born and raised in Atlanta, Georgia, and educated in the Atlanta Public School System. She retired from the Georgia Department of Juvenile Justice. She was named teacher of the year at one of the regional youth detention centers.

She is an itinerant elder in the AMEC and served as a Christian education director, Sunday school teacher, worship leader, and pastor. Mrs. Alexander is also a songwriter and public speaker.

Memberships include Zeta Phi Beta Sorority, National Association of Science Teachers, Georgia Science Teachers Association, Christ Community and Cobb Bethel AME Churches, Gladys Adams Gospel Ensemble, Carolyn Adams Family and Friends Choir, Women for Morris Brown, Correctional Peace Officers Foundation, Georgia State Retirees Association, and Bank of America Advisory Panel.